Thomas Jefferson Builds a Library

"I cannot live without books."
—Thomas Jefferson, 1815

BARB ROSENSTOCK *Illustrated by* JOHN O'BRIEN

CALKINS CREEK
AN IMPRINT OF HIGHLIGHTS
Honesdale, Pennsylvania

For my sister, Diane, the librarian
—BR

For my daughter, Tess
—JO'B

For information about permission to reproduce selections from this book,
please contact permissions@highlights.com.
Calkins Creek
An Imprint of Highlights
815 Church Street
Honesdale, Pennsylvania 18431
Printed in China
ISBN: 978-1-59078-932-2
Library of Congress Control Number: 2013931061
First edition
10 9 8 7 6 5 4 3 2 1
Designed by Robbin Gourley
Production by Margaret Mosomillo
Titles set in Blackadder ITC
Text set in Bulmer MT Std
The illustrations are done in pen and ink (Rapidograph)
and watercolor (Dr. Ph. Martin's Hydrus) on
Strathmore 4-ply Bristol vellum surface.

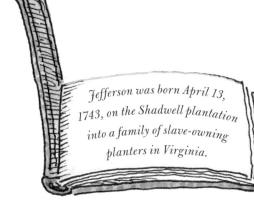

Jefferson was born April 13, 1743, on the Shadwell plantation into a family of slave-owning planters in Virginia.

*T*homas *Jefferson* learned to read. And then, he never stopped. He sat and he read. He walked and he read. And lying in bed, instead of sleeping, he read.

Books, books, books!
Stories and geographies.
Poems, prayers, and plays.

Tom gobbled books the way a starving man eats. Before he turned six, people said he'd read every book in his father's library.

Jefferson's father had a library of forty-nine books, a great luxury in colonial times, that included Salmon's State-Trials, Rapin's History of England, and Anson's Voyage Round the World. Family lore says that young Thomas read all his father's books before starting school.

At school, Tom learned to read Latin. **Amo libros!** ("I love books!") He learned to read French. **J'aime lire!** ("I love to read!") He learned his manners—tripping through the minuet and bowing to the ladies, blushing till his freckles disappeared.

Tom rode, hiked, sang, and played the fiddle,
but he loved reading best. While at college, he read fifteen hours a day.
Guess what he started collecting?!

From about the age of fifteen, Jefferson copied his favorite English, Greek, and Latin passages into his commonplace book.

Thomas Jefferson attended the College of William and Mary for two years before studying law.

Histories and contracts. Medicine, music, and math. Tom bought books on when to plant, where to build, and how to think. Books with paintings, some with maps.

Books from Williamsburg to Philadelphia.

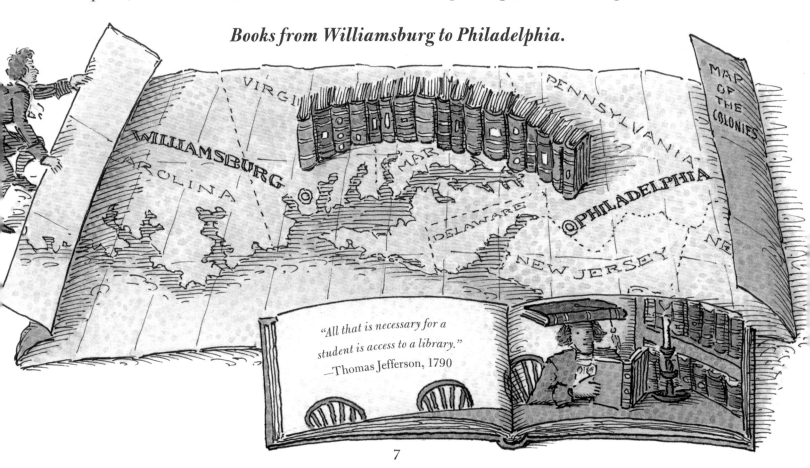

"All that is necessary for a student is access to a library."
—Thomas Jefferson, 1790

Tom married, and he read. He built a house, and he read. And Tom made sure his children read, too.

Two years before Jefferson was married, his first library at his parents' plantation was destroyed in a fire. "Would to god it had been the money; then had it never cost me a sigh."
—Thomas Jefferson, 1770

Jefferson designed his home, Monticello, on a hilltop outside Charlottesville, Virginia. At first, the library was located on the second floor. But later, Jefferson moved it downstairs as part of his private rooms for reading, writing, drawing, and sleeping.

Thomas Jefferson married Martha Wayles Skelton on New Year's Day, 1772. She shared his love of reading and music.

The Jeffersons had six children, but only two daughters, Martha and Mary, survived to adulthood.

He spent weeks organizing books. Huge folios on the bottom shelves, palm-sized duodecimos on top. Books with red, blue, green, or brown covers stacked floor to ceiling. Tom's library wasn't in alphabetical order like others. He grouped books by subject, first in nine broad categories, later in three classifications divided into forty-six different topics. Tom spent hours deciding exactly where each book belonged.

"Old Master had abundance of books: sometimes would have twenty of 'em down on the floor at once: read fust one, then tother."
—Isaac Jefferson, enslaved tinsmith and blacksmith at Monticello

Tom belonged in that library at Monticello. He never wanted to leave his wife, Martha, his children, his farm, or his books. But when the colonists wanted their freedom from England, the people of Virginia needed someone smart to represent them.

Guess who they picked?!

At the Continental Congress in Philadelphia, Tom used all he knew, from all the books he'd read, to write the Declaration of Independence. These words started a new country, the United States of America. Now, many famous folks knew Thomas Jefferson—that tall redhead, standing off in the corner, reading.

Along with his family and schoolmates, Tom included books as his best friends.
Books made him laugh.
They made him wonder.

"My dear Martha—I am anxious to know
what books you read."
—Thomas Jefferson to daughter Martha, 1784

Sometimes, they made him cry . . . as he did in the days he watched hopelessly while his wife grew weak, a new baby girl by her side. Tom sat by her bed, reading the lines they'd copied together from their favorite book, as Martha lay dying.

Tom and Martha's favorite book was The Life and Opinions of Tristram Shandy, Gentleman by Laurence Sterne. Jefferson kept the paper with the lines they had copied from the book, wound with a lock of Martha's hair, for the rest of his life.

In Jefferson's time, books were commonly sold unbound. The pages were then taken to a bookbinder, who stitched and covered the book in the way the owner wanted.

Tom missed Martha. He spent months riding alone in the woods near Monticello. His friends thought work might ease Tom's sadness. His new country needed strong friends in Europe. By fighting for independence, the young United States made many enemies in England. Someone must ask the king of France for help with trade and loans. **Would Mr. Jefferson consider moving to Paris?**

Tom packed his memories and traveled across
the ocean for the first time.

He sailed, and he read.

He bounced in fancy carriages, and he read.

"Books were at all times his chosen companions."
—Ellen Wayles Randolph, granddaughter of Thomas Jefferson

He bowed to the king, charmed the court,
helped his country, and he read.

Guess what Tom saw in Paris?!

The cathedrals, the courts, the queen,
and, of course, the . . .

When he wasn't busy with kings and courtiers, Tom shopped for new books—from Paris, Amsterdam, Frankfurt, Madrid, and London—in languages he knew (English, Latin, Greek, Italian, French, Spanish, Anglo-Saxon) and languages he wished to know (German, Dutch, Bengali, Arabic, and Welsh).

Booksellers loved to see Thomas Jefferson. He bought books from those he liked and those he didn't, in shops or street markets, for pennies or pounds. A few cost more than a working man made in a lifetime.

Tom bought two thousand books in five years, more than a book a day.

"Turning over every book with my own hand."
—Thomas Jefferson, on buying books in Paris, 1814

Ten years after he came home, the people elected Thomas Jefferson the third president of the United States. At that time, the U.S. Congress owned a small reference library of books on law and government. President Jefferson supported this Library of Congress, appointed the first librarian, and suggested books to buy.

In 1805, Jefferson estimated that, in thirty-four years of collecting, he had spent $15,000 on books for his library, more than a quarter of a million dollars in today's money.

15,000.
×16.666
250,000

While president, Tom doubled the size of the country and more than tripled the number of books in its library.

In 1803, during Jefferson's presidency, the government paid France between three and four cents an acre for a tract of land west of the Mississippi. This "Louisiana Purchase" added 828,800 square miles to the United States.

After two terms as president,
Tom retired to Monticello, surrounded
by family, friends, and books.
He added to his house. He worked
in his gardens. He raced his
grandchildren, cuddling them and
reading their hearts.

In his study, Tom used a revolving bookstand to read
five books at a time. His chair and worktable revolved, too, so
he never needed to stop writing to read or stop reading to write.

"When the candles were brought, all was quiet immediately, for
he took up his book to read. . . . Generally we followed his example
and took a book; and I have seen him raise his eyes from his own
book, and look round on the little circle of readers and smile."
—Virginia Randolph Trist, granddaughter of Thomas Jefferson

MEET THE AUTHOR

Thomas Jefferson published two books: Notes on the State of Virginia *and* Manual of Parliamentary Practice.

SCIENCE · HISTORY · STORIES

He wrote at least nineteen thousand letters, many about books. He told people what to read and when—science before noon, history until supper, stories from dark till bedtime. He listed books to read and sent boxes of books as presents. He lent books to James Madison, sold books to James Monroe, and when no one else wanted Ben Franklin's books, Tom bought some.

At that time, books were commonly printed with Roman letters at the bottom of some pages. To identify his books, Jefferson typically added a T before the Roman letter I *(the equivalent of a* J *in Latin).*

T.I.

In 1814, England and the United States were at war again. British soldiers invaded
Washington and set fire to the Capitol. Tom heard the terrible news: They'd burned the Library of
Congress. ***Three thousand precious books, gone forever.***

After fifty years of collecting, Tom owned more books than just about anyone else in America. He couldn't let his country go without a library. **_Guess what he did?!_**

Unusual subjects in Jefferson's library: amputation, fencing, volcanoes, fertilizer, cowpox, beekeeping, weaving, malaria, seashells, and torpedoes

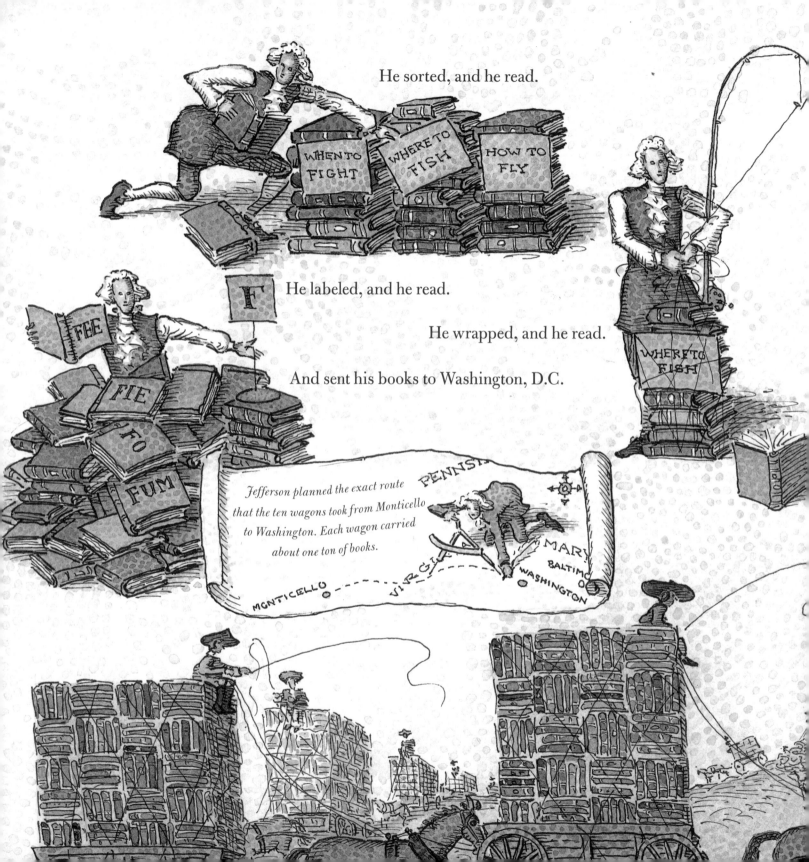

He sorted, and he read.

WHEN TO FIGHT

WHERE TO FISH

HOW TO FLY

He labeled, and he read.

F

He wrapped, and he read.

FEE

FIE

FO

FUM

WHERE TO FISH

And sent his books to Washington, D.C.

Jefferson planned the exact route that the ten wagons took from Monticello to Washington. Each wagon carried about one ton of books.

PENNS[YLVANIA]

MAR[YLAND]

VIRGI[NIA]

MONTICELLO

WASHINGTON

BALTIMO[RE]

"Good, bad, and indifferent, old, new, and worthless, in languages which many can not read, and most ought not."
—Cyrus King, Jefferson political opponent, on Jefferson's books, 1815

Tom's collection of over 6,500 books started a new Library of Congress, more than twice the size of the one lost in the fire. Besides government, politics, and law, Tom's books added a universe of curious subjects. Books on when to fight, where to fish, and how to fly. Microscopes and menus. Games and ghosts. Revolution and remembering.

"I have been 50 years making it, and have spared no pains, opportunity or expense."
—Thomas Jefferson, on his library, 1814

Tom's collection never stopped growing. Two hundred years later, the Library of Congress owns more than **155 million items** on over **800 miles of shelves** in **470 languages**. It adds around **11,500 new items** each day: movies, music, drawings, maps, newspapers, magazines, posters, photos, speeches, and . . .

books, books, books!

Over 35 million books—more than any library ever in history—including this book, the one in your hands.

Like Thomas Jefferson, you are a reader, too.

He'd like that.

Congress paid $23,950 for Jefferson's books—a little more than half what they were worth.

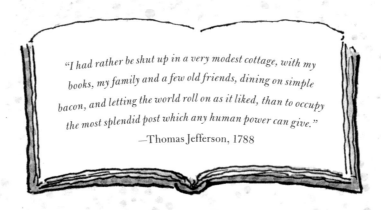

"I had rather be shut up in a very modest cottage, with my books, my family and a few old friends, dining on simple bacon, and letting the world roll on as it liked, than to occupy the most splendid post which any human power can give."
—Thomas Jefferson, 1788

Author's Note

I have remembered Thomas Jefferson and his magnificent library ever since eighth grade, when my class traveled by bus from Illinois to Monticello on a graduation trip. Jefferson collected three major libraries in his lifetime: the first (approximately 300 to 400 volumes) at Shadwell, which was destroyed by fire; the second (nearly 7,000 volumes) at Monticello, most of which he sold to Congress; and the third (1,600 volumes), which he rebuilt during his retirement. Jefferson also maintained a smaller library of more than 700 volumes at his retirement retreat, Poplar Forest, in Bedford County, Virginia.

In 1814, when the British burned the Capitol Building, including the first Library of Congress, Jefferson almost immediately offered his massive personal library to Congress. Angry political debate ignited over whether Congress should buy the books. Jefferson's opponents didn't want the library of their political enemy. Some legislators objected to certain titles as godless, immoral, and useless. Despite the long and heated discussion, Jefferson's unique library was eventually purchased and sent to Washington, D.C., in 1815.

In 1851, a Christmas Eve fire at the Library of Congress destroyed two-thirds of Jefferson's original collection. In 1897, the Library of Congress moved into a larger building (renamed the Thomas Jefferson Building in 1980). Of the books Jefferson originally sold, 2,465 are on display in a permanent exhibit in the Thomas Jefferson Building. In 2010, two researchers from Monticello found more than 80 of Jefferson's books that members of his family had donated to Washington University in St. Louis in 1880. Librarians at the Library of Congress and Monticello continue to search for rare books and pamphlets to someday re-create all the books Jefferson ever owned or read in his lifetime. Hundreds are still missing.

Thomas Jefferson, Slaveholder

From his father, Peter, Thomas Jefferson inherited a library, five thousand acres of land, and about twenty slaves. Over the years, Thomas bought or inherited more slaves through his wife's family and put them to work—planting, harvesting, cooking, cleaning, building, driving, and looking after animals—on his lands. His slaves' labor allowed Thomas Jefferson the time and money to pursue his scientific interests, his book collecting, and his political career.

Thinking about Jefferson today, it seems an impossible contradiction that the same man who wrote the Declaration of Independence, which did so much to advance the cause of human freedom, also denied that freedom to African Americans on the basis of prejudice, custom, and economic interests. Although Jefferson drafted some of the first laws to stop the importation of slaves, often supported the banning of slavery in new territories, and wrote about slavery's evils in letters and essays, he owned about six hundred individuals throughout his life. Many compelling stories of some African American families held in slavery at Monticello can be found at monticello.org/site/plantation-and-slavery.

Acknowledgments

Sincere thanks to Endrina Tay, associate foundation librarian for technical services, and Anna Berkes, research librarian, at Monticello for their profound knowledge of Thomas Jefferson's life and his books. Also thanks to Anne Posega, head of Special Collections, Washington University Libraries, St. Louis, Missouri. And thanks to Donna Somerville of Somerville Design for her design suggestions.

Selected Bibliography and Source Notes*

Basbanes, Nicholas A. *A Gentle Madness: Bibliophiles, Bibliomanes, and the Eternal Passion for Books*. New York: Henry Holt, 1995.

Berkes, Anna. E-mail correspondence with the author, February 2011–June 2012.

Bernstein, R. B. *Thomas Jefferson*. New York: Oxford University Press, 2003.

Brodie, Fawn M. *Thomas Jefferson: An Intimate History*. New York: Norton, 1974.

Jefferson, Isaac, and Charles Campbell. *Memoirs of a Monticello Slave*. Charlottesville: University of Virginia Press, 1951.

Jefferson, Thomas. *The Papers of Thomas Jefferson*. Vols. 1–36. Princeton, NJ: Princeton University Press, 1950–.

Kern, Susan. *The Jeffersons at Shadwell*. New Haven, CT: Yale University Press, 2010.

*Websites active at time of publication

Library of Congress. loc.gov (accessed January 10, 2011–September 15, 2011).

——. *Thomas Jefferson and the World of Books: A Symposium Held at the Library of Congress, September 21, 1976.*
Washington, DC: Library of Congress, 1977.

Malone, Dumas. *Jefferson and His Time.* Vols. 1, 2, 3, and 6. Boston: Little Brown, 1948–1981.

Monticello. monticello.org (accessed January 10, 2011–June 30, 2012).

Peden, William. "A Book Peddler Invades Monticello." *William and Mary Quarterly*, 3rd series, 6, no. 4
(October 1949): 631–636.

——. "Thomas Jefferson: Book-Collector." PhD diss., University of Virginia, 1942.

Randall, Henry S. *Life of Thomas Jefferson.* Vol. 3. New York: Derby and Jackson, 1858.

Randall, Willard Sterne. *Thomas Jefferson: A Life.* New York: Henry Holt, 1993.

Randolph, Sarah N. *The Domestic Life of Thomas Jefferson.* New York: Ungar, 1958.

Sowerby, E. Millicent. *Catalogue of the Library of Thomas Jefferson.* Washington, DC: Library of Congress, 1952–
1959. tjlibraries.monticello.org/tjandreading/libraries.html.

Tay, Endrina. E-mail correspondence with the author, September 2011–June 2012.

Thomas Jefferson's Libraries. tjlibraries.monticello.org (accessed January 10, 2011–September 15, 2011).

Wilson, Douglas L. *Jefferson's Books.* Charlottesville, VA: Thomas Jefferson Foundation, dist. by the University of
North Carolina Press, 1996.

The source of each quotation in this book, listed by page number, is found below.
All books and sources are noted in the bibliography.

Pages 1, 27 (bottom): Library of Congress, Manuscript Division, loc.gov/exhibits/jefferson/images/vc217.jpg;
loc.gov/exhibits/jefferson/images/vc219p1.jpg.

Pages 7, 8, 12, 19, and 30: Jefferson, Thomas, Volume 16 (November 30, 1789–July 4, 1790); Volume 1 (1760–1776);
Volume 6 (May 21, 1781–March 1, 1784); Volume 18 (November 4, 1790–January 24, 1791); Volume 12 (August 7,
1787–March 31, 1788).

Page 9: Jefferson and Campbell, p. 25.

Page 17: Randall, Henry S., p. 345.

Page 22 (top, "reading their hearts" reference): Randolph, p. 345; (bottom): p. 347.

Page 27 (top): Wilson, p. 13.